FOOTPRINTS AND SHADOWS

To my mother, who left footprints for me to follow. Her memory casts a loving shadow on my life.
—AWD

To Peter Holm and Karl V. Larsen
—HS

SIMON & SCHUSTER BOOKS FOR YOUNG READERS
Simon & Schuster Building, Rockefeller Center, 1230 Avenue of the Americas, New York, New York 10020.
Text copyright © 1992 by Anne Wescott Dodd. Illustrations copyright © 1992 by Henri Sorensen.
All rights reserved including the right of reproduction in whole or in part in any form. SIMON & SCHUSTER
BOOKS FOR YOUNG READERS is a trademark of Simon & Schuster.
The text of this book is set in Berkeley Old Style Medium.
The illustrations were done in acrylic.
Designed by Lucille Chomowicz
Manufactured in the United States of America   10 9 8 7 6 5 4 3 2 1
Library of Congress Cataloging-in-Publication Data
Dodd, Anne. Footprints and shadows / by Anne Dodd ; illustrated by Henri Sorensen.   p.   cm.
Summary: Discusses where footprints and shadows go, as when footprints in the snow melt away or shadows
are dispelled by light.   [1. Footprints—Fiction.   2. Shadows—Fiction.]   I. Sorensen, Henri, ill.   II. Title.
PZ7.D685Fo   1992   [E]—dc20   91-46618 CIP   ISBN: 0-671-78716-0

FOOTPRINTS AND SHADOWS

by Anne Wescott Dodd · illustrated by Henri Sorensen

SIMON & SCHUSTER BOOKS FOR YOUNG READERS

Published by Simon & Schuster
New York   London   Toronto   Sydney   Tokyo   Singapore

Where do footprints go?

Footprints in the mud stay put until a gentle rain washes them away.

Footprints come and footprints go.

Footprints in the seaside sand slide away in swirling waves.

Footprints come and footprints go.

Unseen footprints leave a path through fallen leaves. The wind blows, tossing leaves around. And soon no trace of path remains.

Footprints come and footprints go.

Footprints frozen in the snow last a long time in the cold. Then one day the sun's too warm. They simply melt away.

Footprints come and footprints go.

Where do shadows go?

Soft shadows of the tree outside trace moving patterns on the wall. The sun sneaks behind a cloud. The shadows disappear.

Shadows come and shadows go.

Morning shadows start out tall. The hours pass.
The shadows shrink.

Come noon, they can't be found at all.
Shadows come and shadows go.

Long shadows move mysteriously on a moonlit night.

Someone flicks a light on. They quickly run away.
Shadows come and shadows go.

Bedtime shadows at first seem scary, creeping and crawling around
the room. A sleep-tight kiss, a snuggly hug, and they become slow-dancing
shadows, sleepytime friends, settling in to spend the night.
Shadows come and shadows go, never leaving footprints.